THE BIBLE IN SCHOOL.

AN ARGUMENT

Designed to Prove that the Bible is a Necessary Means in the Moral Education of Men, as Members of Society and Citizens of a Free State.

By Hon. J. B. WALKER,

Author of the "The Philosophy of the Plan of Salvation," "Doctrine of the Holy Spirit," Etc., Etc.

CHICAGO:

R. R. M'Cabe & Co., Printers, 57 Washington Street.

1876.

THE BIBLE IN SCHOOL.

Categories of the Reason showing that Revelation is a Necessity in order to the Moral Culture of the Human Mind.

INTRODUCTION.

An attempt is made in the following treatise to show, demonstratively, three things: 1. That the conscience cannot be cultivated without a sense of divine authority; 2. That that authority must be connected with a perfect rule of right; and 3. That the precepts and example of Christ are the absolute and only perfect rule of human conduct. If these propositions are herein proved, then the use of the Bible in schools, in order to conserve and preserve American institutions, is firmly established. And it follows as a necessary inference that the efforts of Dr. William W. Patton, and other able writers, to exclude the Bible from the common school, are unwise and irreligious.

Proposition I.

The species of nature created capable of improvement.

All the higher species of nature, including man, are susceptible of improvement; but no species can advance itself. By the agency of man, individuals of both the vegetable and animal kingdoms may be advanced far beyond what is possible in their natural state. Many species of fruits are "flat, stale, and unprofitable" by nature, and would continue so without the aid of human culture. So the domestic animals have been rendered docile and profitable only by human effort. The statement is verified by all experience, that every being below man that has valuable qualities is capable of improvement; but the culture must come, in all cases, from a nature higher than its own. There are adaptations and dependencies throughout creation between one species and another, but the cultivation which elevates individuals of any species above their natural condition must come from an agency above the species itself. Man is created lord of the animal species. He advances and improves such individuals as are profitable for his use, and destroys others.

In like manner as man is lord of the animal creation, and the only being capable of elevating a species below himself, so, in accordance with the nature of things, the agency of a Superior Mind is necessary in order to the moral elevation of man. Like the lower animals, as we shall see, there is a certain natural level above which man cannot rise without aid from a being superior to himself.

This is true of man especially as a moral being. In intellectual attainment individuals, in some nations, have achieved an advanced position without the aid of revelation. It may be conceded that some of the moral maxims of Confucius, Socrates, and Seneca are similar to those of the Bible; but whatever may be admitted on this point in regard to intellectual attainment, the fact is settled historically that without aid from above himself, man sinks into sensuous vices and cannot attain the moral purity that comes from a true knowledge of God. The Greeks and Romans had many excellent precepts, and advanced intellectually to a high position; but in the knowledge of God and purity of heart they were below many of the barbarous nations by which they were surrounded. The existence of polygamy, of human sacrifices, of lustful worship — the murder of gladiators, and, alas! of the vile and unnatural vice of sodomy, at the period of Rome's highest intellectual attainment, settles the question that mental culture is not moral culture. A people may rise intellectually while moral corruption constantly increases.

Proposition II.

The mental constitution of animals and men indicates the being by whom they must be elevated to a better condition.

The cultivating agent in the case of men, as in that of animals, is easily determined by the mental relations existing between the inferior and superior beings. The mind of animals reaches up to man, and there it stops; it knows no higher lord. It can recognize a man's thoughts, his kindness, and his will, in the relations it sustains to him; and its nature responds by gratitude, obedience, and service. The mind of man, communicated by words and especially by acts, subdues to obedience and elevates to usefulness the animal subjects of his culture. This reveals the natural relation and dependence which God has constituted between the two beings, man and his subjects. These principles apply alike to the relation between the human and the Divine mind. The animal mind reaches up to man and there it stops. The human mind reaches up to God, and there *it* stops — stops naturally, with a sufficient cause. (There may be exceptional minds that doubt about the existence of God; but this comes from looking down through nature to the ultimate of matter, rather than looking up through nature to the ultimate of mind. But the number of such minds that have existed in the world is not so great as the number of monstrosities that have been born with two heads.) A superior mind can look down and understand the constitution of an inferior one better than the inferior can understand itself; but an inferior mind cannot look up and understand a superior one, except so far as the higher mind reveals itself.

Now this created relation between the mind of man and animals, and between the mind of God and man, settles the question with the reason that animals are constituted to obey man, and man is constituted by nature to receive tuition from the superior mind of his Maker; because, as we shall see, it is knowledge of the divine mind and will that produces the cultivation. The thoughts of God communicated by words and acts, are as necessary for the moral advancement of men as like means, by man, are for the advancement of animals. Conformity of the animal to the known will of man constitutes its culture. Precisely the same must be true in regard to man and God. Unless God has constituted relations between himself and His creatures that mean nothing, this view of the relations of man as a being susceptible of culture, to the superior mind of his Maker, is founded in the nature of things. It is not a matter that can be reasonably doubted. We cannot ignore natural relations and adaptations in the creation; and unless we do, we must assent to the conclusion that the mind of man is constituted to receive culture from the superior mind of his Creator. (Man does not cultivate all species of animals, nor all individuals of any species; but the most docile and sagacious both of species and individuals are selected for culture. Is it not so in the moral culture of the human family?)

As, therefore, the mind of man recognizes God, and thereby becomes a subject of divine tuition, the next inquiry in the catenation is: By what means can ideas of the divine character and will be communicated to the human mind?

Proposition III.

Written language the adapted means in promoting the civil and moral progress of men.

A sign language is characteristic of man. Although it may not be developed at the lowest stage of social condition, it is always a necessity as a means of social progress. Animals, to some extent, make sounds and gestures that are intelligible among themselves; but they cannot impress upon matter a permanent sign of their thought. This is an endowment possessed by the human genus alone.

It is not necessary to our argument to discuss the forms of the primitive sign-languages; or whether there were an original language which was the basis of all others. Whether by one method or another, the fact is the same; every settled nation with whose history we are acquainted, formed or possessed a sign-language. As nations advance in age language improves, and the people improve intellectually with the language. Colonies carry the parent language into new regions of the world. In the lapse of time, by the intermingling of peoples, old forms and sounds are modified —some words are lost and new ones admitted; but the attribute of a sign-making and sign-reading being is characteristic of man in all ages, after he leaves the lowest stages of barbarism and attains to a settled habitation. Just as soon as time and settled condition give opportunity, he makes for himself signs of thought; and although the methods may vary, the result is the same—the signs written by the hand of one communicate his thoughts through the eye to the mind of others.

After the language of any people has taken its form, the degree of civilization attained by that nation can be ascertained with perfect accuracy, by the copiousness of their vocabulary, and the shades of discrimination in their definitions. In written language they accumulate and preserve the history, science and sentiment of the past, and add to these the achievements and experiences of the present. Their words, written or engraved, are susceptible of authentication, and thus become the media of commercial and civil transactions; and as law and commerce are conditions of civilization, nothing can be more apparent than the statement that without a written language civilization is impossible. And if civilization is impossible without a sign-language, we cannot suppose that moral culture, which is the crowning excellence of civilization, can be attained without an aid that is necessary to the lower stages of social progress.

Without written language man is a being of undeveloped possibilities—an infant in knowledge while old in years and in crime; a being without purity of heart; living mostly in the present; haunted by demons of imagination; and a prey to human tyrants, as ignorant, but more powerful than himself.

The inquiry then naturally suggests itself whether sign-language is necessary to fix and convey to man not only knowledge of secular things, but knowledge of the Divine character.

Proposition IV.

Sign language the only means by which man obtains a true knowledge of God.

The fact has been shown to be not only historically but philosophically true, that the character of the God in whom man believes determines the moral character of the worshiper; and that man cannot, of himself, attain to a true idea of the divine character. In order to perceive the force of this section a distinct apprehension should be obtained in regard to what man by nature can know and what he cannot know of God. Scripture and experience teach us that from the things that are made man derives the existence and natural attributes of the Maker, *i. e.*, Existence, power and wisdom —"Eternal power and Godhead." (Rom. i. 20; Phil. Plan of Salvation, chap. 1.) A belief in the existence of God has been found in all ages, existing among all races of men; but no two nations, independently of revelation, have had the same idea of the divine character. The diversity in the one case is as perfect as the unity in the other. Without revelation men believe that God is; but their ideas of what He is, are as diverse as their languages. The idea of the divine existence is the idea of being; the idea of character implies quality — comparison. No one can suppose that man has intuitive ideas either of the physical or spiritual qualities of things.

But God cannot have two or more different characters. It follows, therefore, as a logical necessity, that those who conceive of him in a false character, do not worship the true God; and cannot, therefore, receive upon the mind and heart an elevating and purifying influence from the divine character; but, on the contrary, an impression false and injurious.

And just so far as the ideas of different nations differ in

regard to the true God, their imagined symbols and signs of His character will be different. Men were made dependent upon sign-language for advancement, but they had no signs of the divine character that would give either unity or truth to the moral qualities of the object of their worship; and hence, diversity in the conception of the divine character has been universal among all unenlightened nations.

The reason of this failure to derive the character of the true God, without revelation, is obvious. Nature is yet imperfect, and the phenomena of nature differ in different regions. (It is an interesting study to observe with what uniformity the different nations have derived the character of their gods from the peculiar phenomena of the region where they dwell. The gods of the Northmen are heroes of slaughter—of the Southmen of repose and quiescence.) And as all signs of thought originate in the external world and reach the mind through the senses, there is no archetype from which a true and uniform sign of the divine character can be derived. Hence the theologies originated by the human mind in all ages, are now seen by the enlightened reason to be erroneous in conception and debasing in influence. The best thing which unaided men can do is that which they always have done—clothe their ideas of eternal power and godhead with the imperfect attributes of their own nature, and worship the erroneous conception. And even in this respect the idolatries of the masses fell below what reason might have deduced from nature. As, therefore, nature furnished no sign of the true God, the inquiry arises, how could correct ideas of the Divine character be imparted to the human mind?

Proposition V.

Moses was a sign-maker.

We have seen that every nation gave a different character to their gods, and that creation which is yet imperfect could furnish no symbols of the moral attributes of the Creator. Now, if any one says, contrary to this deduction, that man could derive from a knowledge of himself or of his surroundings, perfect righteousness and love — the answer is decisive without argument—Man has never done so in any circumstances or nation. Hence, whether it were possible or not, a revelation by signs or symbols, adapted to communicate knowledge of God, was necessary, or man's ignorance and debasement would have continued.

Now, it is a matter verified by the experience of the Jewish people, that the Old Testament process of revealing by signs the character of Jehovah, is in accordance with the laws of language, and in adaptation to the uncultured state of the elected nation. This is the marked and peculiar character of the Levitical rites. The ritual dispensation was entirely symbolical; and the symbols were signs of first ideas in the knowledge of God. Added to these symbols were principles of law and worship; so that by the working of the Mosaic economy, there were coined, as in a die, the signs which conveyed to the Jewish mind a true conception of the character of God — so far as God was revealed in the introductory dispensation.

Moses was a sign-maker. His mission was understood in the dispensation of which he was mediator. His symbols were given him by vision, and he was required to conform them, in all things, to the patterns revealed to him. (Exodus xxv. 40.) He was instructed to form his signs "according to the pattern showed him in the mount." So the New Testament writers understood the design of this system of signs, and affirm that they are not of earthly origin, "but of things in the heavens." (Hebrews ix. 23.) Thus, by revelation, the righteousness of God, as law-giver, was declared under the Old Testament dispensation ; and the symbols which foreshadowed a further dispensation of truth and mercy were transferred into the Hebrew language, and thus became fixed signs of religious truth. They could thus be understood by those who worshiped at a distance from Jerusalem, where the original symbols were still exhibited. And their significance being thus transferred into written words, the ideas which they conveyed could be transmitted to the future, and translated into other tongues.

In the beginning of the Christian dispensation the same method of producing ideas of the fullness of the Divine mercy was adopted. But we have the substance of the symbolic rites of Moses in the cross of Christ, which gives to believing men a living knowledge of the love of God — a degree of mercy not conceivable before the personal self-sacrifice at Calvary. This central symbol is transferred into the fixed sacramental and written signs of the New Testament, and thereby becomes a permanent element of human culture for all time.

That manifestation was made by sacrifice transformed into symbol, and transferred into the words of sign-language "to be manifested to all in due time." An idea of greater benevolence could not possibly be produced than that exhibited by the excruciating death of the cross for the benefit of others. The possibility, therefore, of revealing the divine love by symbol and sign-language is ultimated in the cross of Christ and the Christian revelation.

Love, the saving element of the divine nature, is thus fully revealed by symbol and sign. Yet this revelation of truth is of no value only so far as men are influenced and actuated thereby. By what means, then, can this objective truth become subjective in the heart and authoritative with the conscience ?

This brings us to the crowning inquiry : By what means can the truth be made efficient to strengthen the conscience and purify the heart, at the same time that it enlightens the intellect? This culture of all the powers of the mind is the only way to produce a symmetrical and useful and therefore noble character. This end all intelligent teachers, patriots, and Christians will seek. How, then, does truth become a life-directing element in the moral culture of the mind ?

Proposition VI.

Truth becomes efficient for moral culture only when the soul sees the authority of God in it.

The soul of man, as demonstrated in Proposition II., is made to recognize God — to recognize the relation which we sustain to Him as a superior being. A sense of this natural relation has exerted a marked influence on mankind in all ages and nations. It is an idea innate in all men. It may be called the God-sense—an impulse which affects men more than any other principle of their nature. Not only the worships, but the wars, the architecture, sculpture, painting, poetry, everything by which man can express the deepest sentiments of the soul, has been produced by the influence of this sense of God in the mind. It has produced different effects in different nations in keeping with their views of the divine character; but it has never failed to move the minds of men, and its effects upon men have been productive of evil in all cases where the truth has not been revealed. If God is just, this natural impulse implies a revelation of truth which, in accordance with the law of progress, "will be manifested to all in due time."

But although truth is a necessity without which the God-sense works evil in the human soul, yet in itself alone truth has no power to elevate man as a moral being. It may enlighten the mind, but it does not quicken the conscience or purify the heart. If knowledge produced virtue, the wisest men would be the best men. But a man may be as intelligent as Borgia, and yet be as base; or as Locke, and yet not be as good. With this innate sense of our relation to God, there must be truth which we recognize as revealing His character and will. Truth authorized and enforced by the God-sense is the only perfect means or media of moral culture. Where man by sin or unbelief has lost this sense of his relation to God, there is no force in the truth that relates to God. The general conception of a father is one thing—to recognize and feel the relation—my father—is quite a different thing. The concrete is life—the abstract is death. A father and Abba Father are so distinct, that one may not affect the conduct in any degree, while the other affects the conscience, the heart, and the will. What, therefore, man needs in order to moral culture, is truth recognized as coming from God—truth in which he recognizes divine authority.

When God has revealed His character and His will, the sense of relation which sees God in truth is usually called faith. This sense, as we have seen, is natural, and exists both in the light and the dark. It gives divine authority to falsehood where the truth is not revealed. In the dark it sees objects indistinctly and in imaginary forms, and affects the mind as that of a child that is impressed by fear and phantoms of the imagination. Not only this, but faith in falsehood will pervert the conscience, as certainly as truth will rectify it. There are Mormons that believe at the same time in the divine mission and licentious doctrines of Brigham Young, and consequently and conscientiously they become almost bestial in their habits. There are men and women who sacrifice themselves or their children to idols, in obedience to some vow which they had made to a supposed supreme being — or to discharge some imagined duty which their faith enjoined. Whatever a man believes to be duty in the sight of his God, he is so made that the conscience enforces obedience. (See John xvi. 8-11, and Ephesians v. 13.) It is made to hear the voice of God; and when a man believes that he hears that voice, conscience will respond to the call, whether true or false. If God is just and good, a revelation of truth is implied both in the nature of faith and in the character of the conscience. The Bible is made for man in the same sense that the Sabbath is; and without it conscience has no life in regard to God, and faith is not a blessing.

This brings us to the final proposition of the series. Before stating this, it will give coherence to the whole catenation if we notice in connection some of the points that have been already established.

As man is endowed with the capacity to exercise faith in a Superior Being; as this sense of revelation moves him to debase his nature by the worship of false gods where the true character of God is not revealed; as that character can only be discovered by divine revelation; and as that revelation can be made only by a sign-language — these conclusions being established, there remains the inquiry whether the written language of the New Testament—whether the divine character as revealed in Christ, be the means, and the only adapted means, of moral culture in the family, the school, and the nation.

In this inquiry, whether we take the theological exposition or the scientific one, it is agreed by all parties that man is capable of culture, and that truth alone is the appliance by which he must be elevated from a barbarous to a higher moral condition. It is agreed, likewise, that the prosperity of individuals, of families, and of the nation depends on the principles of righteousness and love. It is agreed, likewise, whether the means are used by God or men, that there must be special adaptations to accomplish special ends. Assuming these principles and postulates, we reach the last, the key-stone proposition in the series.

PROPOSITION VII.

The Christian revelation alone has specific and perfect adaptations to accomplish the moral culture of men as individuals, as families, and as citizens.

Adaptation 1. It is necessary, in order that man should make progress in morals, that he have some accepted standard of duty, by comparison with which he may be shown his defects in heart and life. No man can make an effort to advance to a higher condition until he sees and feels that his present condition is a low or a wrong one. Conviction of wrong is a necessary antecedent to effort for the right. Until a man sees that his present state is a bad one, he cannot, and ought not, to make an effort for a better. Besides, without a common standard of duty there could be no agreement among men in regard to what is right, and good, and true; and no accepted measure by which virtue and vice could be determined.

Furthermore, the standard of duty must be of such excellence that a man could attain to it only by perfecting all his powers. Persons who believe that they have reached the excellence of their model have no impulse or motive to make advances. The man who strives to copy a perfect picture, although he may fail, will see by comparison where his defects are; while without such a standard, he will neither know his defects nor know when he is advancing to a perfect attainment. It is clear, therefore, that the mind of man is so constituted by its Maker, that a perfect standard of life is necessary in order to the progressive development of his faculties.

This perfect example, likewise, must be a human example (Phil. Plan of Salvation, chap. x). Man's nature could be perfected only by conformity to a model man. We could not follow the example of an angel or of any other being whose faculties were different from our own. And it must be an example of right action in our circumstances. Precept alone is not sufficient. Man needs to understand the application of the precept in his peculiar surroundings, as the denizen of a sinful world. In a world without sin the same law would not require the same duties. We also need to know the spirit of heart in which our duties are to be discharged toward our fellow men. A man may do a good act with a bad spirit, and a right act with a wrong motive. A true life, in spirit and practice, as a standard of duty, is a first and essential need in order to the moral progress of men from a lower to a higher moral condition (Phil. iii. 12-14).

Now, this foundation-stone laid in the New Testament, cannot be moved. The Lord Jesus Christ has given a perfect standard of human duty, conjoined with the spirit in which that duty should be discharged, and empowered the same by Divine authority.

About the perfection ot this standard, no one who believes that God exists, and that man is a sinner, can have any doubt. There can be nothing better in precept or in practice than to love God with all our heart, and our neighbor as ourself. If God himself were to give any other standard, or a standard in any other form, it would have to be a worse one, because it could not be better. Jesus gave this standard in precept, in practice, and in spirit. And as

Christ is perfect, the individual aspiring to that standard will, by assimilation, become more and more so. And as the God-sense is connected with the example so that no one can believe the New Testament, without connecting God with the precept, and as divine favor is promised to all who strive perseveringly, however they may fail, the standard is not only perfect in itself, but it is perfectly adapted to secure, as well as to direct, human effort to the highest attainment. (It is sacrilege to compare the moral standard of Jesus, as some have done, with the most eminent moral characters of the ancient world. Seneca was ostentatious and licentious. Socrates forsook his wife to consort with the harlot Aspasia. Plato's community of women, and vulgar words, repel the pure in heart. *Jesus alone* lived a divine life in a sinful world, and attached the God-sense to his example.)

Adaptation 2. But a general exhibition of truth does not accomplish special ends; it needs to be applied to the distinctive evil propensions of the mind. The evils of the mind, like the diseases of the body, assume specific forms and manifestations. In order to meet these mental habitudes, standard truth must be specifically applied to counteract and remove them.

Selfishness does not always manifest itself in evil action, but more frequently it assumes the character of uncharitable and malignant feeling. The evil and the injury that it inflicts are within the mind itself. The mental constitution is such that any ill-will cherished toward another creates unrest and oftentimes wretchedness. The Savior says, "Love your enemies." This is contrary to nature; but if we disobey, and hate even an enemy, we destroy the peace of the soul. We do not injure the object of our hatred; but we injure ourselves. And so far as malignity predominates the penalty is experienced in the soul. This internal evil is the source of all external guilt. The remedy should therefore be applied to the seat of the disease, and adapted to its character. The prescription of the Great Physician would be adapted to the internal nature of the disease: Notice now the power and application of remedial truth concentrated at this point—"He that is angry with his brother without cause, shall be in danger of the judgment. And whosoever shall say to his brother, Raca [a hard and malignant feeling], shall be in danger of the council. But whosoever shall say, Thou fool [a feeling of malignity and contempt combined], shall be in danger of hell fire. Therefore, if thou bring thy gift to the altar and rememberest that thy brother has aught against thee, leave thy gift before the altar, and go thy way; first be reconciled to thy brother, and then come and offer thy gift" (Matt. v. 22-25).

Every one will remember the numerous and striking instances of the application of truth to an uncharitable heart: "Judge not; for with whatsoever judgment ye judge, ye shall be judged again." "Forgive, when ye stand praying, if ye hope to be forgiven." "Love and pray for your enemies." "Overcome evil with good." Here are precepts which are applied to the source of evil in the mind; and which directly antagonize the evil exercises to which the soul is propense. Some such precepts may be found scattered in isolated sentences in Pagan writers; but nowhere but in the New Testament are they found in absolute forms combined with the God-sense, and their accumulated power applied directly to remove the evils of the heart.

Adaptation 3. But not only the heart, but the will, needs a specific application of truth. When divine precept has availed to abate the evils of the heart, it is not always, nor often, that the benevolent activity is induced, which Christ's example requires. Selfishness is natural and habitual; and, unconsciously, it often perverts the religion of Christ into a religion of mere forms and worship. God needs nothing—not even to be reminded of His glorious attributes. There can be no religion without grateful love to God in Christ: but even "perfect love" without labor for the good of men is not obedience. It is not sufficient; and it may become sinful, in the sense that it is sought selfishly, and is a waste of religious power; not being applied to the will for the good of others. Machinery may be made to operate by steam or any other force, without the power being applied to any useful purpose. And when the steam works the engine without being applied to the boat, it works freely in itself, but it works uselessly; and not for the end designed by the maker.

This form of selfishness which seeks heaven by worship alone — cries Lord, Lord, while we do not the things which Christ's precept and example require — is one of the most subtle and difficult to eradicate from the human heart. It is grounded in indolence, and loves religious forms and ease and respectability for self's sake. The world cannot be converted to Christ until those who profess to be His disciples deny themselves and follow Him in opposing whatever injures man, and in labor for their good. In the reason of the case, therefore, the strongest power of the gospel would bear against selfish religion,— against faith without works.

Is this so in the New Testament? Let us see: The sacrifice of Christ is the strongest power which reaches the soul of the believer. This offering the New Testament declares to be a sacrifice of self for the good of men (1 Pet. iii. 18); even for enemies, to make them friends. The mind can conceive of no greater sacrifice of self on the altar of benevolence. Christ's life, also, was entirely consecrated to labor for the temporal and spiritual good of those in need. And having lived as an example, He says to every one, "Take up your cross daily and follow me." It is duty to pray; and it is pleasant to read and hear essays concerning Christ's character, and human duties. This is not only pleasant, but to many it is profitable. But if Christ's example and precept is the standard, no man is following the Savior in the narrow way who is not prompted to personal labor for man's redemption from ignorance and sin.

In this matter of Christian obedience good men sometimes mislead others. We have just read a little book written by an excellent and able minister, in which he portrays the continued peace of those who exercise faith; and who in all social and business relations maintain a character without offense. This book contains but a single sentence, incidentally expressed, in regard to the duty of personally commending Christ to those in a state of sin. The Christian may find rest if not comfort in such quiescence in the Divine will. This is the ultimate state sought by Brahmaism, Buddhism, and Islamism; but conformity to Christ finds peace and joy, not in quiescence, but in active service for the salvation of men. The state of heart we have noticed may, perhaps, be called piety in the sense of purity; and it is the source from which spiritual impulse should reach the will, but it is not the holiness which Christ's sacrifice and example require. "He died for all, that they that live should not live unto themselves."

First — Even prayer and benevolent desire do not fulfill the requirements of the New Testament without corresponding action. Many people pray that God would relieve the poor, the needy, and the sick,—just as though God personally distributed money and bread and medicine. The inspired teacher says: "If a brother or sister be naked and destitute of daily food, and one of you say unto him, Depart in peace! Be ye warmed and filled! notwithstanding ye give them not those things which are needful to the body — what doth it profit? Even so faith, if it have not works, is dead, being alone."

Second — Man needs specific instruction and urgent impulse at this point to lead him to follow Christ in benevolent labor, without which no precept, no prayer, will redeem men from ignorance and sin. Now, the sacrifice and service of Christ, as written in the New Testament, is a perfect and merciful adaptation to promote the accomplishment of this end: and certainly as faith in Christ's sacrifice and example increases, the world will, in the end, be a brotherhood in Christ.

Adaptation 4. It is necessary, as love and labor are required together in Christian life, that the love of the Lawgiver should be manifested in connection with his will. As faith without works is dead, so works without love are dead.

(Heb. vi. 1.) But the manifestation of love by the Lawgiver is the only thing that can beget love in those to whom the law is given. Everything begets its kind—love begets love. Love is both a reconciling and a propulsive power. It desires to give the precept that will benefit others, while it manifests the affection that reconciles them to obedience. Hence, law and love are one in Christ. ("God Revealed," Book 2, Chap. 1). He revealed the law by His life and precept, at the same time that He revealed love by His life and sacrifice. No man can believe in Christ's life without believing in His law; nor in His death without believing in His love. Law and love unite in His ministrations. To love God in Christ, is to love the Lawgiver; and love to the Lawgiver is the only religious impulse to obedience. The New Testament inculcates the service of a son, not of a servant. "The law came by Moses, but love and truth by Jesus Christ."

Adaptation 5. But there are two tables of the law—one requiring love to God as the Lawgiver; the other love to man as a neighbor and brother. We are required to labor for man as the end and aim of religious life; but we are required to labor for him as a brother, in obedience to God as a Father.

The law, therefore, requires generic love to man—that is, love to man as man, and action for individuals according to their needs. A mother loves all her children alike; but if one is sick, or in danger, she neglects all the others,—perhaps she does not even think of them,—to attend to the wants of the needy one. And every father who loves his son will endeavor to form the character of that son into accordance with his highest ideal of human character. But the world furnished no standard of the true man, any more than it did a standard of the true God. Men had lost the knowledge of both the true God and the true man. Heroism, philosophy, intellect, wealth, power, are the earthly estimates of "the highest style of man." But to love the character of man as thus exhibited, is to corrupt the mind, and mislead effort by a false standard.

How, then, shall we know what man's character ought to be in a sinful world, in order that we may labor to conform others to that standard and labor in accordance with their needs? The answer to this inquiry shows not only the whole law fulfilled in Christ, but presents Christ in special and blessed adaptation to man's nature and his wants. Consecration to Christ produces love to God and man at the same time. God and man were united in His person. In loving Him we love the true God as He is, and the true man as he should be. When Christ becomes the standard of character and duty in any mind, labor, from the very nature of love and reason, will be directed to make others like Him. Thus, in loving Christ, we love the true God and the true man in one. We obey both tables of the law at the same time; and we obey the law as the will of the Lawgiver.

The following propositions have been proved *seriatim:*

1. Man by nature is a cultivator, and is himself capable of cultivation.

2. No species can raise itself above its natural level, but must be elevated by a nature superior to its own.

3. The mental constitution of animals and man shows that man is the cultivator of nature, and that God is the cultivator of man.

4. Written or sign language is the only adapted means of elevating man from a barbarous to a civilized state.

5. Nature furnished no signs of ideas that would reveal the true character of God.

6. Moses was a sign-maker; and in the New Testament the cross of Christ is the ultimate sign of divine love.

7. Truth in written language has, of itself, no power to change moral character. It may enlighten the intellect, but a sense of God in truth alone gives the efficacy to reach the heart and conscience.

8. The Christian revelation in the New Testament has the characteristics which are specially adapted to the moral culture of mankind.

9. Special adaptations of the New Testament, which show the agency of God as distinctly as adaptations in nature.

These conclusions being legitimately established, it follows—

First—That to exclude the Bible from the common schools is a crime against families and against the state, because it withholds the only efficient means of cultivating the moral faculties of the children, upon which depends order and law and progress in society and in the state. The action of the legislature or school board, therefore, is suicidal that rejects the Bible as the standard authority of morals in the school-room.

Second—Any effort made by sects, or churches, or skeptics to accomplish the exclusion of the New Testament should be resisted by every patriot. *The New Testament is not sectarian. Its history and morals are equally received by all sects.* A government founded on the will of the people can stand only on the intelligence and conscience of the people; and conscience can be rectified and empowered only by faith in Divine Revelation; the man, therefore, who aids ignorant or superstitious men of any sect to exclude from the schools that culture which gives light to the mind and rectitude to the conscience of the voter, and raises him above the influence of the bigot and the demagogue, should be enlightened as an ignorant man, or resisted as an enemy to free government.

Third—It is not the amount of the Scripture read, or the particular version that the teacher may use, which is important in the case. It is the divine authority that the nature of the child needs. This alone meets the appetency of a mind that reaches up to God. Prayer, recognizing God and His will, as revealed in the New Testament, would aid to make the life and precepts of Christ the standard of duty in the mind of the pupil. Thus by the effect of the Bible upon the teacher and the scholar our schools would become a beneficient power, developing both the intellectual and moral faculties of the rising generation. Upon this the stability and prosperity of the great American republic depend.

The moral necessity urged in the foregoing argument for

the use of the Bible in school will avail against all objections that can be alleged against it. If it be admitted that conscience culture of the citizen is necessary in order to the stability and prosperity of the republic, and that the God-sense in connection with truth alone has power to guide and quicken the conscience, then necessity which knows no objection, demands the use of the Bible, because it is in this country the only recognized divine teaching.

It should be noticed, however, that many of the objections alleged are irrelevant, or they do not see the vital principle in the case. The regard that some would pay to the conscience of the Papist, the Mormon or the Chinese would lead them to make the common schools godless rather than impinge upon the convictions of the superstitious, the vicious, or the pagan. Such a course would be a public recognition of superstition, Mormonism and heathenism as equal with Christian morals. It would foster a difference among citizens in regard to the proper standard of duty, and cherish the most malignant and hurtful of all social alienations — religious dissension. To educate the people at the cost of the state in the common schools without a common standard of morals is to encourage them to perpetuate their own diverse standards, or to reject all standards of duty.

Differences of opinion with regard to books and parts of the Bible do not affect the vital principle, which requires truth, with the God-sense. There may be parts and books of the Bible which in our time are profitless. Some parts of the Old and imperfect dispensation may be unfit to be read in school; but no one, either Jew or Gentile, will object to the moral teaching of the Ten Commandments and the Sermon on the Mount. Selections from the Bible are used as elements of moral culture, as select lessons in reading and examples in arithemetic are used as elements of intellectual culture. And in fitting children for citizens of a free state the one is as necessary as the other. The Bible is not a sectarian book — even the objection to the version can be obviated by the use of the Lord's Prayer and lessons from the Sermon on the Mount, which are essentially the same in all versions.

It has been said, let the schools be godless and Christians will give Bible instruction at home. But that is to say professing Christian families alone should be qualified for citizenship, while it is the ignorant foreign and native population that need the aid of both intellectual and Bible culture. The professing Christian families in the country that would read the Bible to their children are probably not one in fifty of the whole population.

The Bible always has been the badge of Protestantism. The common school, with the vital principle of the God-sense involved, was the chief legacy of those Protestants who originated our free institutions. They established as part and preservative of our democratic institutions — "Free schools for all and the Bible in school," as the hope of national prosperity. Is it wise, after an experience of the value of their legacy, in promoting the public good, to inaugurate godless schools for those to whom we transmit the interests of the future for time and eternity?

While it might be expected that some who oppose all acknowledgment of God by oath, assent, or worship, would be in favor of godless schools, we see not how a Christian can be so. The precept which he himself accepts as the rule of duty requires the teaching of Bible truth as the "saving health" of the individual and of the public mind. The precept is not to give Bible instruction only to one's own family, but to "teach all nations." To believe the Christian Scriptures and not favor all proper ways to disseminate knowledge of Christ's precepts, as authority in matters of duty, is contrary both to the principle and the practice of the Christian religion. Let the New Testament, without comment, be read in the school, and if any parent wishes to give sectarian or even anti-christian instruction at home (which will not be true of one in a hundred), this is a free land, and each parent — Christian, Mormon, or Chinese, has control in his own house, but not in schools sustained by the state. There, if morals are taught at all, one only standard with the God-sense attached is a necessity.

www.ingramcontent.com/pod-product-compliance
Lightning Source LLC
LaVergne TN
LVHW011145110826
845150LV00008B/2515
* 9 7 8 1 4 1 8 1 9 2 3 6 5 *